THE
BRITISH
MUSEUM Pocket Dictionary

HEROES &
HEROINES
OF ANCIENT GREECE

Richard Woff

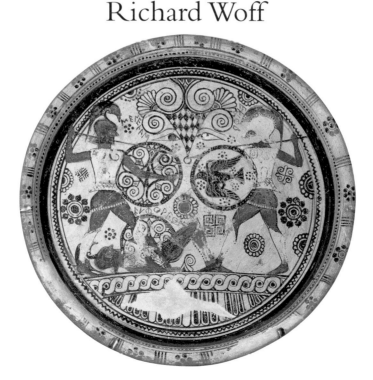

THE BRITISH MUSEUM PRESS

© 2004 The Trustees of The British Museum

Published in 2004 by
The British Museum Press
A division of
The British Museum Company Ltd
46 Bloomsbury Street,
London WC1B 3QQ

ISBN 07141 3103 2

Richard Woff has asserted his right to be
identified as the author of this work.

A catalogue record for this title is available
from the British Library.

Designed and typeset by
Peter Bailey for Proof Books
Cover designed by Herring Bone Design

All photographs are taken by the British
Museum Photography and Imaging
Department, the British Museum, except p38,
photography © 2004 Museum of Fine Arts,
Boston; p18 (top), p21, p40, p42, © J. Paul
Getty Museum, Malibu, California; p48 ©
James Watson.

Heroes and heroines were the central
characters in many traditional ancient
Greek stories. More than that, they
were role models for how to behave
or how not to behave. They were also
often worshipped like gods and
respected as the founders of cities and
ethnic groups.

CONTENTS

A–Z index of heroes and heroines

Heracles

Heracles was the greatest of all Greek heroes. He was so great that he eventually became a god. Heracles' father was Zeus, king of the gods, but his mother was an ordinary human. For this reason, Hera, wife of Zeus, hated Heracles and persecuted him cruelly. When he was just a baby, Hera sent two snakes to kill him, but Heracles strangled them to death. When he grew up, he married happily and had a fine family. Hera then sent a cloud of madness on him and he killed his wife and children.

Hercules was the Roman name for the Greek Heracles. This Roman bust of Hercules is probably based on a bronze statue made in Greece 500 years earlier.

Heracles

As a punishment, he became the slave of his cousin King Eurystheus of Tiryns, who set him twelve tasks or labours to complete. His first labour was to kill a fearsome lion whose skin was so tough that ordinary weapons could not pierce it. Heracles wrestled the lion and choked it to death. He then used the lion's claws to cut the skin and after that he wore the skin as armour. His second labour was to kill a snaky monster called the hydra which had many heads. Every time Heracles cut off a head, three more grew. He had a clever idea and asked a friend to help him – every time he cut off a head, the friend burned the stump to stop another one growing. Finally Heracles struck off the final head and the monster was dead.

Several cities in the Greek world claimed Heracles as their founder. This coin is from Heraclea in southern Italy and shows Heracles fighting the lion.

Heracles' third and fourth labours were to capture a fierce wild boar and a swift footed deer which had bronze hooves and gold antlers. Next, he had to kill some bronze-feathered birds which had infested the area near a lake. Heracles used a rattle to scare the birds into the sky and then shot them with his bow and arrows. For his sixth labour he was sent to Elis. King Augeas of Elis owned huge herds of cattle and their sheds had never been cleaned. Heracles changed the direction of a nearby river so that it flowed right through the sheds and washed away the mountains of manure.

On this pot from ancient Athens, Heracles uses a bow and arrows and a club to attack the hydra. These were his favourite weapons.

Heracles

Heracles' seventh labour was to capture a huge bull in Crete. This he did and brought it back to Greece. He then had to seize some ferocious flesh-eating horses from a cruel king – Heracles fed the king to his own horses and after that they became tame.

For his final four labours Heracles was sent to the furthest corners of Greece and beyond. First he had to go far to the north and bring back to Eurystheus the belt of the queen of the Amazons. Then he went to the distant west and killed Geryon, a three-bodied giant. His eleventh labour was to go down to the Underworld and bring back Cerberus, the multi-headed dog which guarded the gates to the land of the dead.

An ivory statuette of Heracles wrestling the Cretan bull. It was made in the first century AD.

8

Finally, he again went to the furthest west, where the sun sets, to fetch the golden apples from the Garden of the Hesperides. Only the huge titan Atlas was allowed to get the apples and his job was to hold up the sky on his shoulders. Heracles released Atlas by taking the sky on his own shoulders. When Atlas returned with the apples he refused to take the sky back, but Heracles tricked him. He asked Atlas just to hold the sky for a moment while he adjusted his lion skin. When Atlas foolishly agreed, Heracles picked up the apples and left. By completing this final labour, Heracles had won his freedom at last.

Both during and after his labours, Heracles had many other adventures. These included trying to steal the sacred tripod from Apollo's temple at Delphi, serving a queen as a slave by doing women's work, fighting with centaurs, attacking Troy and defeating monsters and bandits of many different kinds.

Here Heracles gets the apples of the Hesperides himself without asking Atlas. Notice the snake guarding the tree.

Heracles becomes a god. This tiny scene from the
lip of a drinking cup shows Athena bringing
Heracles to his father Zeus.

After completing his labours, Heracles married again and had several children.
His new wife was Deianira and Heracles had rescued her from a fierce centaur
who was trying to carry her off. Heracles shot the centaur with his bow. With his
dying words, the centaur told Deianira that his blood was a powerful love-charm,
so she smeared a robe with the blood and kept it safe in case she should ever
need it. Some years later, Deianira learned that Heracles had fallen in love with
another woman. In an attempt to win Heracles back to her, she sent him the
blood-stained robe as a present. But the centaur had tricked her and his blood
was a terrible poison which ate away Heracles' flesh when he put on the robe.
Dying, Heracles climbed up on a funeral pyre he had built on the top of a
mountain. A friend set the pyre on fire and the mortal Heracles was burned away.
Athena carried away the immortal hero and brought him to his father Zeus on
Mount Olympus. There, Heracles was reconciled with Hera. He was given Hebe,
the goddess of youth, as his wife and took his rightful place among the gods.

Peleus

Peleus was king of Phthia in the north of Greece. His wife was the sea goddess Thetis. Zeus, king of the gods, loved Thetis, but received a prophecy that her child would be greater than its father, so he decided that she had to marry a mortal.

Thetis resisted the men who came to try to take her in marriage by changing shape so that they could not capture her. But Peleus was a skilful wrestler and he held on to her no matter what form she took: snake, lion, fish or water itself. Finally he overcame Thetis and they had a huge wedding to which all the gods and goddesses came.

Their son was Achilles, but they did not have a happy marriage. Thetis spent most of her time living in the sea with her father's family. Achilles was killed at Troy. Peleus grew old alone.

Nobody knows for sure, but some experts think that this glass vase shows Peleus on the left and Thetis with a sea serpent.

See also Achilles page 43

Atalanta

Atalanta was the closest a Greek woman ever came to being the same sort of hero as the men.

When she was a baby, her parents left her out to die in the hills. A she-bear found her and brought her up as her cub. Atalanta grew up brave and strong, a very fast runner and a skilful hunter. She was one of the Argonauts who sailed with Jason and also took part in a famous boar hunt with other Greek heroes.

Atalanta did none of the usual things Greek women did. She would only marry the man who could beat her at a running race and no-one could do that. Finally, a man named Hippomenes challenged her, but every time Atalanta overtook him, he threw down a golden apple. Atalanta slowed down to pick up the wonderful apples and lost the race. Hippomenes won the race and forced Atalanta to marry him.

A Roman mosaic from Halicarnassus in Turkey. Atalanta is out hunting with her spear and bow and arrows.

12

Meleager

Meleager was son of the king of Calydon in northern Greece. When he was born, the Fates said that he would live until a branch then burning in the fireplace turned to ashes. His mother snatched the branch from the fire, put it out and kept it safe in a box.

Meleager hunts a leopard on this mosaic. You can see his name written in Greek above his swirling cloak.

Meleager grew up into a strong young man and a great hunter. One day, a ferocious boar was ravaging the lands of his father, so Meleager gathered together a band of the best hunters to kill it. Among this band was Atalanta. Meleager fell in love with her and when the boar was killed awarded her its tusks. When his uncles protested that they should have the tusks, Meleager attacked and killed them.

When Meleager's mother heard that he had killed her brothers, she took out the branch and threw it back into the fire. All Meleager's strength and life drained away.

Oedipus

Oedipus' greatness and downfall lay in his intelligence. While running away from his home in Corinth, he got into an argument with a man and killed him.

He then came to Thebes where he found the city plagued by a monster called the Sphinx. She had the head of a woman and the body of a lion. She posed her victims a riddle which none could answer and then killed them. The riddle asked which animal has four, two and three feet? The answer is *humans*: they crawl as babies, walk as adults and use a stick when they are old. Oedipus solved the riddle and killed her. As a reward for freeing Thebes, he was made king and married the widowed queen. Later, after they had had four children together, Oedipus uncovered the truth: the man he had killed was his real father, the king of Thebes, and the woman he had married was his mother. Afflicted with horror at what he had done, Oedipus blinded himself and, accompanied by one of his daughters, left Thebes for ever.

In the eighteenth century, the British artist John Flaxman drew this illustration for a play which Sophocles wrote about Oedipus' death. It shows Oedipus with his daughters.

Daedalus and Icarus

Daedalus was a very skilful craftsman. He was from Athens, but had come with his son Icarus to live at the palace of King Minos of Crete. There he made a maze called the Labyrinth at the centre of which lived the Minotaur, a horrible monster, half–bull, half–man.

When Minos would not let Daedalus leave Crete, Daedalus made some wings for himself and his son out of wax and feathers. Before they set off, he warned Icarus not to fly too near the sun. As the two made their escape through the sky, Icarus enjoyed

Wealthy Romans had their houses decorated with paintings showing popular stories. This painting from Pompeii shows Icarus plummeting towards the sea.

flying so much that he forgot his father's words. He flew higher and higher until the heat of the sun melted the wax and the boy plummeted to his death in the sea below.

Daedalus never returned to Athens but settled instead in Sicily or Italy.

Medea

To an ancient Greek man, Medea was a threat in every way. She was a woman, she was foreign and she did magic.

She was the daughter of Aietes, king of Colchis. When Jason arrived to try to steal the Golden Fleece, Medea fell in love with him. She showed him where the fleece was and used magic to drug the dragon that guarded it. She then helped Jason escape by cutting up her own brother to slow down the pursuing Aietes.

When they reached Greece, Medea helped Jason defeat his wicked uncle. They settled down together and had two children. Some time later, Jason decided to marry a Greek princess. Furious, Medea sent the princess a dress smeared in a poison which burned her flesh when she put it on. Then, to Jason's horror, Medea killed their children and flew away to Athens in a chariot drawn by snakes.

Medea defeated Jason's uncle by magically changing an old ram into a young one by boiling it in a cauldron. When the uncle got in, Medea boiled him to death.

Orpheus

Orpheus' music could soothe wild animals, make trees follow him and stop rivers flowing.

One day Orpheus' wife Eurydice was bitten by a poisonous snake and died. Orpheus followed her down to the Underworld where he charmed asleep the fearsome three-headed dog that guarded the entrance. Even Hades and Persephone, king and queen of the dead, were softened by his music and agreed to let him take Eurydice back to the upper world as long as he did not look at her until they reached the light of day. They were a few steps away from sunlight, when Orpheus could resist no longer, looked back and lost her for ever.

Orpheus, overcome with grief, wandered the mountains where he met some women maddened by the god Dionysus. The women tore him apart and threw his head into a river. Still singing, it was washed down to the sea.

Orpheus sits on a rock singing as he plays his lyre. The two warriors are wearing cloaks and hats from Thrace (modern Bulgaria and northern Greece).

Helen

Helen was the daughter of a mortal woman and Zeus, king of the gods, who made love to the woman in the form of a swan. Helen and her sister Clytemnestra were born from eggs.

Helen was the most beautiful woman in the world, but also the most destructive. She was married to Menelaus, king of Sparta. When the Trojan prince Paris visited Sparta, they fell in love and ran away together to Troy. Menelaus appealed for help to his brother Agamemnon and a Greek army set out to recover Helen.

This bronze strip was used to decorate the strap of a shield. Menelaos leads Helen away from Troy by the wrist. On the right Athena watches.

The two figures on the left seem to be about to climb aboard a ship. Might this be Paris taking Helen off to Troy?

When Troy was captured, Menelaus found Helen in the ruins. In anger at the death and pain she had caused, he drew his sword, but saw her beauty and could not kill her. In one version of her story, it was a phantom of her which went to Troy and the real Helen spent the war in Egypt.

Paris

Paris was a son of Priam, king of Troy. Knowing that Paris would bring destruction upon Troy, Priam had the baby put out in the hills to die. Paris was taken in by shepherds and grew up to be very handsome.

One day, as Paris was tending the flocks, the god Hermes led up three goddesses and told him that he had to settle an argument by judging which of them was the most beautiful. The goddesses tried to bribe Paris: Hera and Athena offered him power and wisdom; Aphrodite offered him Helen of Sparta, the most beautiful woman in the world. Paris chose Aphrodite. Eventually, Paris rejoined his family in Troy and on a visit to Greece stole away Helen and started the Trojan War.

As Paris guards his sheep in the mountains, the three goddesses approach. Hera brings the prize – a golden apple.

Paris was not a brave warrior and preferred the bow to the spear and sword. With his bow he killed the mighty Achilles.

19

Circe

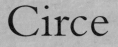

Circe was a witch who lived in a palace on a thickly-wooded island. Whenever strangers arrived on the island she would welcome them into her palace and then change them into animals using a magical potion.

This drinking cup was used during secret religious rituals. Circe brings a cup of magic potion to try to turn Odysseus into a pig.

Her most famous guest was Odysseus who arrived with his men on the way back from Troy. Circe succeeded in changing some of Odysseus's men into pigs, but when she tried to do the same to Odysseus himself she found that he was protected by a magic plant given to him by the god Hermes.

Odysseus forced Circe to release his men from her spell and then lived with her on the island for a time. She gave him advice about how to reach the Underworld and about how to avoid other dangers on his way home to Ithaca.

20

See also Odysseus page 31

Penelope

Penelope was the wife of Odysseus. While Odysseus was away fighting at Troy, she remained at home looking after his aged father and their young son. After the war, when all the other Greeks had returned home, the noblemen of Ithaca pestered Penelope to marry one of them so he could become king. They even took over the palace, where they acted insolently towards those who remained faithful to Odysseus.

Penelope delayed her decision by saying that as soon as she had finished weaving a funeral cloth for Odysseus' father, she would marry one of the suitors. However, whatever she wove during the day, she unpicked at night. Eventually, Odysseus arrived home and killed the suitors in a fierce battle. Penelope used one more trick to make Odysseus reveal a secret known only to them. Now that she was sure her husband had really returned, she came to his arms.

While her son Telemachos sleeps, Penelope unravels the weaving she has done during the day. Joseph Wright of Derby painted this in 1783-4.

Perseus

Perseus came from Argos. His grandfather, Acrisius, received a prophecy that his grandson would kill him, so he locked up his daughter Danae in a room where no man could reach her. However, Acrisius had not reckoned with Zeus, king of the gods, who came to Danae in the form of a shower of gold. When Perseus was born, Acrisius had the baby and his mother shut up in a box and thrown into the sea. They were rescued by a fisherman and Perseus grew up to be a strong young man.

The local king wanted Danae as his wife and decided to get rid of Perseus by sending him on an impossible mission. He told Perseus to bring him the head of the gorgon Medusa, a fearful monster whose glance turned people to stone.

Perseus has Medusa's head in his bag and takes off in his winged sandals. Athena is there to help him.

Helped by Athena and Hermes, Perseus obtained four gifts to complete his task. These were a curved sword, winged boots, a cap of invisibility and a special bag to hold the head. In some versions of the story Perseus cut off Medusa's head by looking in a mirror so that he would not be turned to stone by her eyes. His winged boots helped him escape from the other two gorgons who chased him after their sister's death cries awoke them.

Perseus used the head to help him rescue the princess Andromeda from a sea monster. Next he killed the wicked king and rescued his mother. He then gave the head to Athena to wear to terrify her enemies. At last, with Andromeda as his wife, he

Andromeda was an Ethiopian princess. Here, two attendants support her as she waits to be fed to the horrible sea monster.

returned home to Argos. His cruel grandfather had run away, but some years later Perseus killed him by accident during an athletics contest. Perseus left Argos for Asia, where he gave his name to the Persian people.

Bellerophon

This bronze container was made by the Etruscans who lived in central Italy. It shows Bellerophon with Pegasus on the left.

Bellerophon was from Corinth, but lived for a time at the court of the king of Argos. When the king learned that his wife had fallen in love with Bellerophon, he sent him away to the king of Lycia in what is now southern Turkey. He gave Bellerophon a secret letter to give to the Lycian king asking the king to put him to death.

Instead of killing him, the king sent Bellerophon to fight a terrifying monster called the chimaera. The chimaera was a lion in front, a dragon at the rear, a goat in the middle and breathed fire. Athena gave Bellerophon a bridle with which he tamed the winged horse Pegasus. Riding Pegasus, Bellerophon killed the chimaera after a fierce fight. The king of Lycia realized that Bellerophon was a very special young man and gave him his daughter as wife and half of his kingdom.

Theseus

Theseus was the son of Aegeus, king of Athens, and the greatest Athenian hero.

He was born and brought up in Troezen along the coast from Athens. His mother showed him a large rock and told him that when he was strong enough to lift it, he would be ready to go to Athens to meet his father for the first time and to claim his birthright. When he eventually lifted the rock he found beneath it a sword and a pair of sandals. Taking these, he set off on the coast road to Athens.

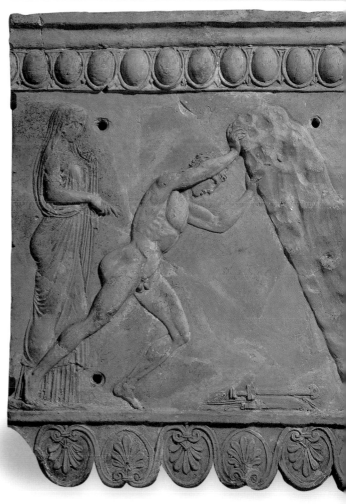

Theseus lifts the rock to discover the sword and sandals left there by his father.

Inside this Athenian drinking cup, the painter has shown all the adventures of Theseus on his way to Athens. See how many you can recognize!

On the way he had several adventures. First he met and killed a robber and took his club to use. Next he came across Sinis, who tied his victims to two bent-over pine-trees, which he released, tearing them apart. Theseus did the same to him. After killing a fierce flesh-eating pig, he killed Skiron, a robber who forced travellers to wash his feet and then kicked them over a cliff to a flesh-eating turtle. He defeated a powerful wrestler and then came to the house of Procrustes. This evil bandit welcomed guests to his home and offered them a bed for the night. If they were too short for the bed, he stretched them, if they were too long, he cut them down to size. Theseus made Procrustes lie on his own bed. Procrustes was too long, so Theseus cut off his head.

Theseus

When Theseus arrived in Athens, he narrowly escaped being poisoned by the witch Medea, who had taken refuge with Aegeus. Fortunately, his father realized who he was and drove Medea from his palace. Theseus arrived just in time to try to save Athens from a terrible payment demanded by Minos, king of Crete, as punishment for the murder of his son on Athenian land. Every year the Athenians had to send seven young women and seven young men to Crete to be fed to the Minotaur, a horrible monster in the form of a powerful man with the head of a bull. Theseus insisted that his father allow him to go to Crete as one of the young men. His father agreed reluctantly, but told Theseus that if he returned from Crete alive, he should change the sails of his ship from black to white.

The Minotaur does not look very terrifying here as Theseus prepares to kill him with his sword.

A Cretan acrobat leaps over a charging bull. Bulls were very important to the people of ancient Crete. This may explain the origin of the story of the Minotaur.

In Crete, Ariadne, daughter of Minos, helped Theseus kill the Minotaur. Then he and his thirteen companions, along with Ariadne, set sail for home. On the way back to Athens, Theseus abandoned Ariadne on the island of Naxos. As Theseus's ship approached Athens, he forgot his promise to his father and did not change the colour of his sails. Aegeus, who was watching from the cliffs, threw himself into the sea in despair. This is how the Aegean Sea was given its name.

Theseus ruled Athens well. He united his country and defended it against the Amazons, whose queen he married. He was less happy in his private life and his second wife, Phaedra, and his son Hippolytus died in unhappy circumstances. Eventually, he grew less popular and left Athens. It was said that he was murdered on the island of Scyrus. In about 475 BC, the Athenian general Cimon brought Theseus' bones back from Scyrus to Athens for burial.

See also Ariadne page 36

Jason

Jason's father was king of Iolcus in the north of Greece, but Jason's uncle, Pelias, had driven the rightful king from the throne. Pelias sent Jason on an impossible quest. In Colchis, on the coast of the Black Sea, there was a marvellous object: a ram's fleece made of pure gold. Jason's challenge was to bring back this Golden Fleece. Helped by Athena, Jason had the very first ship built, the Argo. He assembled a crew of heroes including Heracles, Peleus, Orpheus and Atalanta. They were called the Argonauts.

The Argonauts had many adventures during the voyage. They rescued a blind king who was being persecuted by the Harpies, terrible winged monsters which snatched away his food. They had to sail between two huge rocks which clashed together destroying anything between them. Jason sent a dove through so that he could judge exactly when the rocks came together. At the right moment Jason urged his men to row with all their strength and the Argo slipped between the rocks with just a little damage to its stern.

The ship-builder Argo gets help from the goddess Athena in building the first ever ship.

In this drawing by the seventeenth-century Italian artist Pietro da Cortona, Orpheus has charmed a fierce dragon to sleep so that Jason can take the Golden Fleece.

When the Argonauts reached Colchis, the king, Aietes, agreed to hand over the Golden Fleece if Jason could yoke two fire-breathing bulls and plough a field. When he accomplished this feat, Aietes made Jason sow dragon's teeth in the furrows. From the teeth sprang huge armed warriors. Jason defeated them by throwing a stone in their midst so that they began to fight among themselves.

Aietes planned to ambush and murder the Argonauts the next day, but his daughter Medea had fallen in love with Jason. Medea helped Jason to get the fleece and to escape from Colchis. When Jason, Medea and the surviving Argonauts arrived back at Iolcus, Medea tricked Pelias' daughters into killing him and Jason became king.

Odysseus

Odysseus was king of the island of Ithaca and always preferred cleverness to brute force. His grandfather was Autolycus, the Master Thief, son of the god Hermes. He was one of the goddess Athena's favourite heroes.

Odysseus' intelligence brought him much success and he did not hesitate to use tricks, to steal and to cheat to get what he wanted. He could also be reckless and often put his men in danger.

When Agamemnon came to recruit Odysseus for the war against Troy, Odysseus pretended he was mad. He yoked together a horse and an ox and started to plough the earth and sow salt. His trick was uncovered when someone put his baby son in the way of the plough and Odysseus turned aside to avoid hurting him.

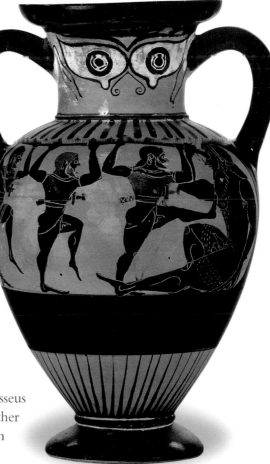

Odysseus puts his foot against the Cyclops' chest as he and his men blind him with a wooden stake.

Odysseus

At Troy, Odysseus did his fair share of fighting and even volunteered to face Hector in single combat. But it was his cunning that was the greatest threat to the Trojans. He took part in ambushes and, disguised as a beggar, entered Troy to spy on the Trojans. He stole the statue of Athena on which the safety of Troy depended and it was his idea to build the wooden horse, hide Greek warriors inside and then trick the Trojans into taking it into their city.

After the destruction of Troy, Odysseus set off for home with his men. They raided an island on the way and then were driven by a storm to the land of the lotus-eaters. After eating the lotus-fruit, many of his men forgot their home and Odysseus had to drag them back on board by force. Next, he arrived on the island of the one-eyed giants called Cyclopes. One Cyclops, Polyphemus, shut Odysseus and his men in his cave and proceeded to eat them. Odysseus got Polyphemus drunk and while he was asleep blinded him with a red-hot wooden stake. When the Cyclops let his sheep out of the cave, Odysseus and his men hid underneath them and escaped. Odysseus could not resist taunting Polyphemus, who asked his father the god Poseidon to avenge his blinding.

The sea monster Scylla had a snaky body and dogs' heads sprouting from her waist.

Odysseus' ship sails past the sirens. Odysseus is tied to the mast
so he can hear their song and survive.

Next Odysseus arrived at the island of an enchantress named Circe. He managed
to overcome her powers and she gave him directions to the Underworld. There,
Odysseus met the ghosts of some of his friends who had died at Troy and of his
dead mother, and learned how he himself would meet his death. After leaving
the Underworld, Odysseus sailed between Charybdis, a fearful whirlpool, and
Scylla, a sea monster who snatched men from ships as they passed by. He also
had to get past the Sirens, whose song was so beautiful that sailors couldn't resist
it and were shipwrecked on the jagged rocks that surrounded their island.
Odysseus ordered his men to tie him tightly to the mast of his ship so that he
could not go overboard. Then they filled their own ears with wax. In this way,
he became the only man to hear the Sirens' song and survive.

After his final shipwreck, Odysseus was washed ashore
naked and alone. Here he asks for help from the
princess Nausicaa.

Poseidon eventually avenged the blinding of Polyphemus by shipwrecking
Odysseus naked and alone on the island of a nymph named Calypso. He stayed
there for several years, but finally set off for home on a raft. After another storm
he was washed ashore on an island whose kindly king and queen took him in
and sent him back to Ithaca on one of their ships. There, he joined forces with
his son and killed the men who had been living in his palace and harassing his
wife Penelope. Finally, after twenty years away, Odysseus had come home and
was re-united with his faithful wife.

Aeneas

Son of a Trojan prince and the goddess Aphrodite, Aeneas was a great fighter, but it was not for his feats in war that he became best known.

The Greeks captured Troy by hiding in a wooden horse which they tricked the Trojans into bringing inside the city walls. Amidst all the death and destruction, Aeneas realized that he could not save his city. Instead he gathered together his family and some followers. Then, holding his son by the hand and carrying his aged father on his back, he set off from Troy to find a new future.

Aeneas' travels took him far and wide across the Mediterranean and he almost settled in Carthage (in what is now Tunisia), where he fell in love with Dido, queen of Carthage. In the end he arrived in Italy and built a new life there. His descendants were to become the Romans.

This Roman coin shows Aeneas leaving Troy with his father on his shoulders and leading his son by the hand.

Ariadne

Ariadne was daughter of Minos, king of Crete. When Theseus came to Crete to try to kill the Minotaur, a terrible bull-headed monster, Ariadne fell in love with him and decided to help him. The Minotaur lived in a maze called the Labyrinth, from which it was impossible to find your way out. Ariadne gave Theseus a ball of thread and explained that he should let it out as he entered the maze and then follow it back again after killing the Minotaur.

The nineteenth-century British artist Edward Burne-Jones painted this watercolour for a book of flowers. Ariadne sits with her ball of thread and the Labyrinth in the background.

The plan worked perfectly and Ariadne and Theseus set sail back to Athens. They arrived at the island of Naxos where they rested for the night. The next morning Theseus sailed away leaving Ariadne asleep on the beach. Some say he abandoned her deliberately, others that he simply forgot her. Happily for Ariadne, the god Dionysus discovered her on the island and made her his wife.

See also Theseus page 25

Phaedra and Hippolytus

Theseus' first wife was Hippolyta, the Amazon queen. Their son was Hippolytus. After Hippolyta died, Theseus married Phaedra, sister of Ariadne.

Hippolytus grew up into a handsome young man and was a keen hunter and follower of the goddess Artemis. The goddess Aphrodite made Phaedra fall in love with Hippolytus. When Phaedra told him of her feelings, the young man was shocked and rejected her angrily. Phaedra, overcome with shame, killed herself, but left a letter for Theseus accusing Hippolytus of being in love with her. Theseus was furious, banished Hippolytus and put a curse upon him. As Hippolytus drove his chariot along the seashore away from Athens, a huge bull appeared from the sea and panicked his horses. The young man was thrown to his death.

This painting of Phaedra looking anxious was on the wall of a room in a house in Pompeii when the city was destroyed in AD79.

37

See also Theseus page 25

Agamemnon and

Agamemnon was king of Argos and
Mycenae and the leader of the
Greeks who fought at Troy.
When the Greek army had
gathered at Aulis to set sail to
Troy, the goddess Artemis refused
to let the wind blow unless
Agamemnon sacrificed his eldest
daughter Iphigenia to her.
Agamemnon tricked his daughter into
coming to Aulis by pretending that she
was to marry Achilles. After he had
sacrificed her, the wind began to blow
and the Greeks were able to leave.

During the Trojan War the god Apollo forced
Agamemnon to give back a Trojan woman he had
captured after a battle. He claimed Achilles'
woman instead and a great argument
followed which nearly caused the Greeks
to lose the war.

Agamemnon's wife was Clytemnestra,
daughter of Zeus and twin sister of Helen.

Clytemnestra

While Agamemnon was away at Troy, she behaved very differently from Penelope, the wife of Odysseus. Clytemnestra hated Agamemnon for sacrificing their daughter, so during his absence she took a lover, Aegisthus, and together they ruled the kingdom.

When Agamemnon returned home, Clytemnestra greeted him in a friendly way, spread out rich cloths for him to walk over into his palace and prepared him a luxurious bath. Once Agamemnon was in the bath and defenceless, Clytemnestra and Aegisthus killed him.

Aegisthus murders Agamemnon who is wrapped in a cloth to prevent him resisting. Clytemnestra strides in from the left with an axe.

Electra and Orestes

This bronze figure was probably attached to a wooden chest. It may show Orestes stepping forward to kill his mother Clytemnestra.

Electra and Orestes were the younger children of Agamemnon and Clytemnestra. When Clytemnestra murdered Agamemnon, Orestes was smuggled away to safety by one of his father's faithful servants. Electra remained at the palace, but was terribly unhappy. She missed her brother and hated her mother.

Eventually, Orestes returned home in secret with his friend Pylades and was re-united with his sister. Together they planned revenge for their father's murder. With Electra's help, Orestes killed their mother and her lover. He was then pursued by terrifying Furies who were intent on punishing him. He fled all over Greece and even to the coast of the Black Sea, but finally arrived at Delphi where he took refuge at the temple of Apollo. He was sent for trial to Athens where he was released from punishment by the casting vote of Athena and returned to Argos. Electra married Pylades.

Iphigenia

Iphigenia was the eldest daughter of Agamemnon and Clytemnestra. Her father sacrificed her to the goddess Artemis to secure a wind to take the Greek army to Troy, but at the moment of sacrifice, Artemis snatched her away and replaced her with a deer. Artemis carried off Iphigenia to the land of the Taurians, far away from Greece on the coast of the Black Sea.

There, Iphigenia became priestess at Artemis's temple. It was a Taurian custom that the priestess should sacrifice to the goddess any strangers who arrived there. More than twenty years later, her brother Orestes, who had been a baby when she was sacrificed, arrived in the land of the Taurians. He was fleeing from the Furies who were pursuing him for the murder of Clytemnestra. Iphigenia was supposed to sacrifice him, but she recognized her brother. Together, they escaped from the Taurians and returned to Greece.

Agamemnon stands by an altar and raises the knife to sacrifice Iphigenia. We can see both the young princess and the deer.

Seven against Thebes

After the downfall of Oedipus, his two sons Polyneices and Eteocles argued about who should be king. Eventually, Eteocles took the throne by force and drove out his brother. Polyneices fled to Argos, where he married the king's daughter and persuaded his father-in-law to help him gather together an army to win back Thebes. Polyneices recruited six other warriors to fight with him. These were the Seven against Thebes.

The city of Thebes had seven gates and when the army arrived there, the Seven found that each gate was protected by a Theban champion. A great battle followed, but the Seven were unable to capture the city. Polyneices made for the gate defended by Eteocles and there the two brothers killed each other. Eteocles' body was recovered by the Thebans and given a proper burial. Polyneices' body was left on the battlefield for the birds and dogs.

This pot by a Greek-Italian painter shows Capaneus, one of the Seven, attempting to climb the walls of Thebes. Eteocles looks down from the city wall.

Achilles

Achilles was the son of Peleus and the sea-goddess Thetis. When Achilles was a baby, Thetis dipped him in one of the rivers of the Underworld to make him immortal. But she held him by the heel and the water did not touch him there. Thetis knew that Achilles would die if he went to the Trojan War so she tried to protect him by disguising him as a girl. However, Odysseus tricked Achilles into revealing his true identity.

At Troy, Achilles was by far the best Greek warrior. After an argument with Agamemnon, he withdrew from the fighting and only returned when his best friend Patroclus was killed by Hector. He fought and killed many fine warriors including Penthesilea, queen of the Amazons, Memnon and Hector himself. Finally Achilles was killed by Paris, who shot him with an arrow in his unprotected heel.

A silver coin from southern Italy showing Achilles. It was made to honour the Greek king Pyrrhus, who believed his family was connected to Achilles.

Hector

A son of Priam, king of Troy, Hector was the greatest Trojan warrior and the main defender of his city against the Greeks. Homer shows us another side of Hector. As Hector sets out for battle, his wife comes up carrying their baby son. She hands the baby to Hector, but when the child sees his father's gleaming helmet and its tall horsehair plume, he starts to cry. Hector takes off the helmet, cuddles his son and shares a smile with his wife.

After Achilles withdrew from battle, the Greeks would have been defeated by Hector if Patroclus, Achilles' best friend, had not entered the fighting and rallied them. However, Hector killed Patroclus and brought Achilles back into battle. The two great warriors faced each other beneath the walls of Troy. When the god Apollo deserted Hector, Achilles, guided by the goddess Athena, killed the last hope of the Trojans.

Hector on the right goes into battle against Menelaus, husband of Helen. They are fighting over the fallen body of a Greek warrior.

Ajax

There were two heroes called Ajax and both of them fought at Troy. The Lesser Ajax was a mighty fighter, but violent and insolent.

The Greater Ajax was also a stubborn and determined fighter. After the death of Achilles, he was clearly the best surviving Greek warrior and claimed that he should be given Achilles' weapons and armour. However, Odysseus made the same claim. The Greek warriors asked their Trojan prisoners which of the heroes had done them the most damage. When the Trojans replied that it had been Odysseus, the Greeks awarded the weapons to him.

Ajax went mad with anger and, tricked by the goddess Hera, slaughtered a flock of sheep believing that they were the Greeks. When Ajax came to his senses and realized what he had tried to do, he could not live with the shame and committed suicide by falling on his own sword.

This bronze mirror was made by an Etruscan artist. It shows Ajax getting into his armour ready for battle.

45

Amazon Queens

Achilles plunges his spear into the throat of Penthesilea. She collapses, overpowered by Achilles. Her spearpoint dangles in the empty air.

The Amazons were a tribe of warrior women who lived in the far north of Greece. Battles between Greek warriors and Amazons appear in many Greek stories, sculptures and paintings. The two most famous Amazon queens were Hippolyta and Penthesilea.

Hippolyta led the Amazons when they raided Athenian territory. The Athenians, led by Theseus, succeeded in defeating the Amazons and Theseus took Hippolyta as his wife. They had a son called Hippolytus, who was killed because of a curse put on him by his father.

Penthesilea was queen during the War of Troy, when the Amazons came to fight on the Trojan side. Achilles was the only Greek warrior who was able to defeat her. He faced her in single combat. At the very moment when he struck the death-blow, his eyes met hers and they fell in love, but it was too late and she died in his arms.

Memnon

Memnon was the king of the Ethiopians, who fought on the Trojan side in the War of Troy. He was very similar to Achilles in that he was a great warrior and was also son of a goddess. Memnon's mother was Eos, goddess of dawn. She fell in love with a mortal man and carried him off to be her husband.

Only Achilles was strong enough to defeat Memnon. The story of Memnon's exploits at Troy and of his death at the hands of Achilles was told in a long poem called *The Aithiopis* which is now lost.

After Memnon's death, his mother carried his body back to Ethiopia where she wept over him. All his followers were turned to birds and even now, as the sun rises, the birds fly up into the sky and mourn for their dead king. His mother's tears are the dew of morning.

Armed with a sword, Memnon leaps forward against Achilles.
The mothers of the two heroes look on in fear, their arms
stretched out towards their sons.

The Marathonomachai

In the sixth century BC, the Greek cities on the coast of what is now Turkey came under the control of the Persian Empire. In 499 BC, they rebelled against the Persians and were helped by some of the cities on mainland Greece, including Athens. Darius, the Persian king, regained control of the Greek cities, but never forgave Athens for helping them.

In 490 BC, Darius sent a large army to Greece to punish Athens. A much smaller army of Athenians and some allies defeated the Persians at the battle of Marathon. 192 Athenians and 6400 Persians died. The Athenians broke their usual practice and buried their dead on the battlefield under a large mound of earth instead of bringing them home to Athens. For many years afterwards, the Athenians paid their respects to these Marathon-fighters by making offerings at their tomb and they became symbols of Athenian pride and bravery.

The burial mound of the Athenians still stands on the plain of Marathon. Some experts think the Marathon-fighters were also commemorated by the great Parthenon temple on the acropolis in Athens.